To: _____

From: _____

A baby was born in a stable
while a bright star shone down from above,
And the world learned the depth of God's mercy
and the comfort and strength of His love.
May the thought of that long-ago Christmas
and the meaning it's sure to impart
Bring a wonderful message of comfort
and a deep, new peace to your heart.

THE HELEN STEINER RICE FOUNDATION

When someone does a kindness
it always seems to me
That's the way God up in heaven
would like us all to be . . .

Whatever the celebration, whatever the day, whatever the event, whatever the occasion, Helen Steiner Rice possessed the ability to express the appropriate feeling for that particular moment. A happening became happier, a sentiment more sentimental, a memory more memorable because of her deep sensitivity and ability to put into understandable language the emotion being experienced. Her positive attitude, her concern for others, and her love of God are identifiable threads woven into her life, her work . . . and even her death.

Prior to Mrs. Rice's passing, she established the Helen Steiner Rice Foundation, a nonprofit corporation that awards grants to worthy charitable programs assisting the elderly and the needy. Royalties from the sale of this book will add to the financial capabilities of the Helen Steiner Rice Foundation. Because of limited resources, the foundation presently limits grants to qualified charitable programs in Lorain, Ohio, where Helen Steiner Rice was born, and Greater Cincinnati, Ohio, where Mrs. Rice lived and worked most of her life. Hopefully in the future, resources will be of sufficient size that broader geographical areas may be considered in the awarding of grants.

Because of her foresight, caring, and deep conviction of sharing, Helen Steiner Rice continues to touch a countless number of lives through foundation grants and through her inspirational poetry.

Thank you for your assistance in helping to keep Helen's dream alive and growing.

ANDREA E. CORNETT, ADMINISTRATOR

AN OLD-TIME
CHRISTMAS

Helen Steiner Rice & Virginia J. Ruehlmann

Published by Fleming H. Revell
a division of Baker Book House Company
P.O. Box 6287, Grand Rapids, MI 49516-6287

Printed in the United States of America

Library of Congress Cataloging-in-Publication Data

Rice, Helen Steiner.
  An old-time Christmas / Helen Steiner Rice and Virginia J. Ruehlmann.
    p.   cm.
  ISBN 0-8007-1744-9
  1. Christmas—Poetry. 2. Christian poetry, American. 3. Christmas.
I. Ruehlmann, Virginia J. II. Title.
PS3568.I28043   1997
811'.54—dc21   97-15594

Sincere appreciation is hereby expressed to the families of Florence Doogan Juergens and Anna von Dûren Doogan for the use of Christmas cards from their antique card collection; Eileen Annest for use of her portrait of Helen Steiner Rice; Gibson Greetings, Inc., and Eileen Annest for permission to use her artwork on pages 1, 5, 8, 10, 12, 18, 24, 26, 30, 33, 60, 65, 69, 70, 72, 75, and 83; and Rick and Virginia Ruehlmann for use of craft ideas from *Making Family Memories,* published by Baker Book House.

Dedicated to Helen Steiner Rice,

a woman with vision, integrity, compassion,

faith, hope, love, and a God-given talent

to inspire and encourage others

Helen Steiner Rice portrait by Eileen Annest,
celebrating the 75th birthday of Mrs. Rice, May 19, 1975

Gott, sei
mir gnädig
nach
deiner Güte,
und tilge meine
Sünden nach
deiner grossen
Barmherzigkeit.
Psalm 51, 3.

CONTENTS

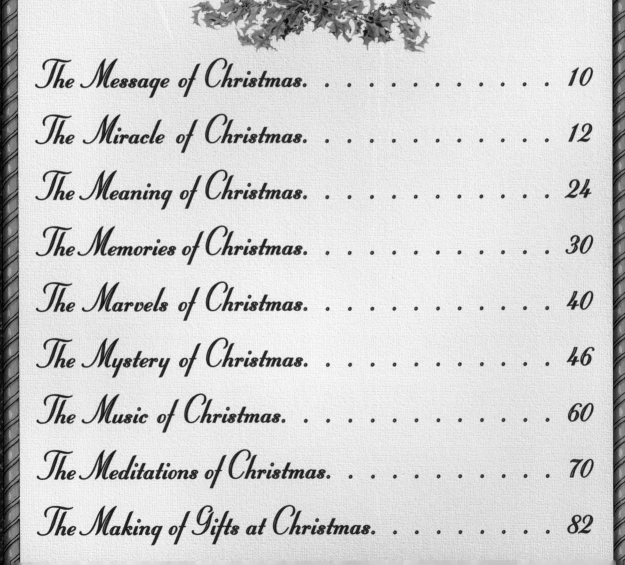

Introduction

The religious significance of Christmas makes this season a memorable, unforgettable, and cherished time of the year. Expressions of love, peace, faith, goodwill, and generosity are also associated with this holy period. These qualities have found expression and interpretation in a variety of forms such as religious ceremonies, decorations, songs, greetings, and traditional practices.

There is a timeless quality surrounding Christmas. Some of the customary practices have been passed down through the centuries, while others are of a more recent development. Victorians supplied a new dimension to the holiday season by popularizing the decorated Christmas tree and the festive excitement of caroling from house to house, as well as rediscovering ancient carols.

The carols, celebrations, customs, gifts, and traditions of long ago continue to warm, charm, and add to the flavor and enjoyment of the holiday season. No doubt, Christmases of the past and those of our times will enhance and be remembered in the future.

The central focus of Christmas is to appreciate, honor, and pay tribute to God's generous gift of His Son, our Savior. God's compassionate gift was gloriously wrapped in love. Helen Steiner Rice emphasized the reason for the season—the birth of Jesus Christ—and captured the message of peace, faith, hope, and love in her poetry. May this collection increase these very qualities in your life and add to your appreciation and enjoyment of the Christmas holidays. May you and yours enjoy many blessed Christmases and many holy, healthy, and happy New Years.

Sincerely,

Virginia J. Ruehlmann

The Message of Christmas

May the message that came
on that holy, silent night
Fill your heart with joy and peace
and make your Christmas bright.

And it came to pass in those days, that there went out a decree from Caesar Augustus, that all the world should be taxed. (And this taxing was first made when Cyrenius was governor of Syria.) And all went to be taxed, every one into his own city. And Joseph also went up from Galilee, out of the city of Nazareth, into Judaea, unto the city of David, which is called Bethlehem; (because he was of the house and lineage of David:) to be taxed with Mary his espoused wife, being great

The Birth of Jesus

with child. And so it was, that, while they were there, the days were accomplished that she should be delivered. And she brought forth her firstborn son, and wrapped him in swaddling clothes, and laid him in a manger; because there was no room for them in the inn. And there were in the same country shepherds abiding in the field, keeping watch over their flock by night. And, lo, the angel of the Lord came upon them, and the glory of the Lord shone round about them: and they were sore afraid. And the angel said unto them, Fear not: for, behold, I bring you good tidings of great joy, which shall be to all people. For unto you is born this day in the city of David a Saviour, which is Christ the Lord. And this shall be a sign unto you; Ye shall find the babe wrapped in swaddling clothes, lying in a manger. And suddenly there was with the angel a multitude of the heavenly host praising God, and saying, Glory to God in the highest, and on earth peace, good will toward men.

LUKE 2:1–14 KJV

The Miracle of Christmas

One element of the miraculous nature of the Christmas story rests in the fact that God utilized the simple faith, devotion, and commitment of ordinary human beings to bring forth unusual and miraculous happenings. The shepherds, the wise men, the innkeeper, Elizabeth, Mary, Joseph, and a host of others were well cast in this spectacular event of the ages. Each had an unexpected part to play in the miracle of the Christmas story. Directed and produced by God the Father, it remains the pageant of the ages.

The Miracle of Christmas

Miracles are marvels that defy all explanation,
And Christmas is a miracle and not just a celebration.
For when the true significance of this so-called Christmas story
Penetrates the minds of men and transforms them with its glory,
Then only will rebellious man, so hate-torn with dissension,
Behold his adversaries with a broader new dimension.
For we can only live in peace when we learn to love each other
And accept all human beings with the compassion of a brother.

THE BLESSINGS

The blessings of Christmas are many,
more than words can express,

Enough to fill every longing heart
with untold happiness.

And the greatest of all blessings
is the Christmas revelation

That Jesus Christ was born this day
to bring the world salvation.

Tell me not that miracles
don't happen anymore;

They happen in believing hearts,
just as they did before.

And it takes the Christ of Christmas
to change our point of view,

For only through the Christ Child
can we all be born anew.

OF CHRISTMAS

And that is why God sent His Son
as a Christmas gift of love,

So that wickedness and hatred,
which the world had so much of,

Could find another outlet
by following Christ's way

And discovering a new power
that violence can't outweigh,

For in the Christmas story
of the holy Christ Child's birth

Is the answer to a better world
and goodwill and peace on earth.

That is why this message
is sent to you to say

That you are wished the blessings
of this holy Christmas Day.

CHRISTMAS
GREETING

THE CHRISTMAS STAR

Christmas Joy
to all

As Christmas dawns
    on a world forlorn
May it dawn in our hearts
    why Christ was born,
And may the full significance,
    like the Christmas star so bright,
Illuminate the minds of all
    with God's truth and love and light.

THE CHRISTMAS STORY

A HAPPY CHRISTMASTIDE

Christmas is more than a dramatized tradition—
it's God's promise to all men
That only through the Christ Child
can we be born again.
It's God's assurance of a future
beyond all that we have dreamed,
For Jesus lived on earth and died
so that we might be redeemed.
Mankind's hope and salvation
are in the Christmas story,
For in these words there are revealed
God's greatness and His glory.

THIS IS THE SAVIOR

All the world has heard the story
    of the little Christ Child's birth,
But too few have felt the meaning
    of His mission here on earth.
Some regard the Christmas story
    as something beautiful to hear,
A lovely Christmas custom
    that we celebrate each year,
But it is more than just a story
    told to make our hearts rejoice—
It's our Father up in heaven speaking
    through the Christ Child's voice,
Telling us of heavenly kingdoms
    that He has prepared above
For all who trust His mercy
    and live only for His love,
For only through the Christ Child
    can we be born again,
For God sent the Baby Jesus
    as the Savior of all men.

Christmas Greetings

May the glow of Christmastide Brighten all the year beside.

For us today, what does this mean—
Just a season with a bright and happy scene?
A gift, a greeting of good cheer?
The ending of another year?
How little we have understood
The meaning as we really should.
Our minds and hearts have been so small,
That we never got the real meaning at all,
For in these tidings, we've all received
Much more than we have ever conceived,
For in these words, beyond all seeing,
"We live, and move, and have our being."

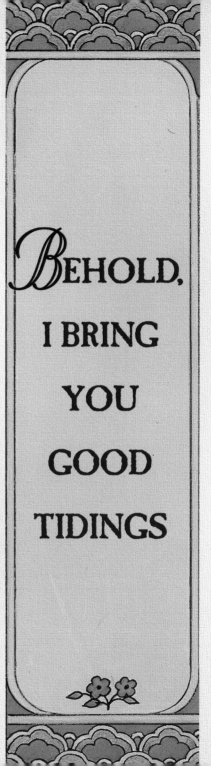

BEHOLD, I BRING YOU GOOD TIDINGS

PEACE ON EARTH

Christmas is God's pattern for living,
To be followed all year by unselfish giving,
For the holiday season awakens good cheer
And draws us closer to those we hold dear,
And we open our hearts and find it is good
To live among men as we always should.
But as soon as the tinsel is stripped from the tree,
The spirit of Christmas fades silently
Into the background of daily routine
And is lost in the whirl of life's busy scene,
And all unaware, we miss and forego
The greatest blessing mankind can know,
For if we lived Christmas each day as we should
And made it our aim to always do good,
We'd find the lost key to meaningful living
That comes not from getting but unselfish giving,
And we'd know the great joy of peace upon earth,
Which was the real purpose of our Savior's birth,
For in the glad tidings of the first Christmas night,
God showed us the way and the truth and the light.

God So Loved the World

Our Father up in heaven,
    long, long years ago,
Looked down in His great mercy
    upon the earth below
And saw that folks were lonely
    and lost in deep despair,
And so He said, "I'll send My Son
    to walk among them there
So they can hear Him speaking
    and feel His nearness too,
And see the many miracles
    that faith alone can do.
For I know it will be easier
    to believe and understand
If they can see and talk to Him
    and touch His healing hand."
So whenever we have troubles
    and we're overcome by cares,
We can take them all to Jesus
    for He understands our prayers,

For He too lived and suffered
    in a world much like our own,
And no one can know the sorrow
    that Jesus Christ has known.
And whatever we endure on earth
    is so very, very small
When compared to God's beloved Son,
    who was sent to save us all.
And the blessed reassurance
    that He lived much as we do
Is a source of strength and comfort,
    and it gives us courage too.
And that is why on Christmas
    God sent His only Son
To teach mankind the wonder
    of the words "Thy will be done,"
And through the countless ages,
    the holy Christ Child's birth
Is our promise of salvation
    and our hope of peace on earth.

The Christ Child

"Let not your heart be troubled,"
　　for on this holy Christmas Day,
God sent the little Christ Child
　　to take our sins away.
And all our heavy burdens
　　became easier to bear
When Jesus told the people
　　God is always there to share
All our trials and troubles—
　　for nothing is too much
When our heavy load is lightened
　　by the holy Father's touch.

CHRISTMAS
GREETINGS

What Is Christmas?

Is it just a day at the end of the year—
A season of joy, merrymaking, and cheer?
Is it people and presents and glittering trees?
Oh no, it is more than any of these,
For under the tinsel and hidden from sight
Is the promise and meaning of that first Christmas night
When the shepherds stood in wondered awe
And felt transformed by what they saw.
So let us not in our search for pleasure
Forego our right to this priceless treasure,
For Christmas is still a God-given day,
So let us remember to keep it that way.

The Meaning of Christmas

Like the watching shepherds
and the wise men Christmas night
May we be guided by the star
that still is shining bright.

CHRISTMAS

Here's to the season
Of good-will and joy
Heres to the Christmas
Thats dawning.

Here's to your health
And may nothing destroy
The pleasures I wish you
this morning.

C-104

The Christ Child's Birth

In our Christmas celebrations of merriment and mirth,
Let us not forget the miracle of the holy Christ Child's birth.
For in our festivities it is easy to lose sight
Of the Baby in the manger and that holy, silent night.

With Best
Christmas Wishes.

MAKE US AWARE

God, make us aware that
in Thy name
The holy Christ Child
humbly came
To live on earth and
leave behind
New faith and hope
for all mankind,
And make us aware that
the Christmas story
Is everyone's promise
of eternal glory.

A MERRY
CHRISTMAS

Unto Us
A Child
Is Born

God sent the little Christ Child
many centuries ago
To walk and talk with mortals
on this sinful earth below,
And remember that God's purpose
in sending us His Son
Was to purchase our salvation
when our life on earth is done.
So let us try to follow
in His footsteps day by day
By loving more and hating less
all those who pass our way.

Let us remember
when our faith is running low,
Christ is more than just a figure
wrapped in an ethereal glow.
For He came and dwelled among us
and He knows our every need,
And He loves and understands us
and forgives each sinful deed.

God's Plan

He was crucified and buried
and rose again in glory,
And His promise of salvation
makes the wondrous Christmas story
An abiding reassurance
that the little Christ Child's birth
Was the beautiful beginning
of God's plan for peace on earth.

Christmas
Wishes

The Memories of Christmas

Memories grow more meaningful with every passing year,
More precious and more beautiful, more treasured and more dear.

CALENDAR

CHRISTMASTIME IS MEMORY TIME

Seasons come and
seasons go
    and with them
    comes the thought
Of all the happy
memories
    the passing days
    have brought—
And looking back
across the year
    it's a joy to
    reminisce,

For memory opens
wide the door
    on holidays
    like this.

31

CELEBRATIONS AND CUSTOMS

Christmas Joy and Happiness

Christmas festivities and customs of bygone years, perpetuated in our society today, add to the numerous and pleasurable aspects of the Christmases of the present. Frequently the origins of customs of long ago have dissolved with time, but the customs, in their continuation, have retained value and honor. They in turn provide a window into and a bond with the past.

The Nativity Scene

It was in 1223 that Francis of Assisi, a friar known today as St. Francis, introduced in the town of Greccio, Italy, the first re-creation of the nativity scene.

St. Francis was concerned that the basic aspects of the Christmas story were not appreciated or fully comprehended by the majority of the people. Sustaining a deep desire to depict the humble birth of Christ in a simple and understandable manner so that all people could grasp the significance of the event, this dedicated friar, with assistance from a wealthy patron, assembled the necessary items, including a life-sized figure of the Christ Child, live animals, a manger, and straw. He asked friends to play the roles of Mary, Joseph, shepherds, and the three kings. Worshipers flocked to this first nativity reproduction. It was an event that was to become an annual tradition during the Christmas season, reproduced not only in churches and communities but also in homes throughout the world.

The nativity scene is known by various names throughout the world. In Italy it is known as the Praesepe; in France, the Creche; in Germany, the Krippe; in Spain, the Nacimiento; in Bavarian regions, the Putz. Whether the display is elaborate or simple and whatever name is used, the Christmas nativity scene results in a deeper appreciation of the birth of the Christ Child.

THE CHRISTMAS TREE

A Joyful Yuletide

All to the good, all be merry
Let the Christmas Tree shine bright;
Midst Mistletoe and Holly berry
Let it indeed be Christmas night!

C-136

Although it is unknown where or when the Christmas tree originated, credit is often given to Germany. The honor of popularizing the decorated Christmas tree, however, belongs to Queen Victoria and her German husband, Prince Albert. An 1848 English engraving features the royal couple and their children admiring their family Christmas tree, decorated by the royal chef with fancy cakes, candies, candles, fruits, and nuts. An American women's magazine, Godey's Lady's Book, published a version of the elaborately trimmed tree of this famous couple in its 1850 edition.

The decorated Christmas tree became fashionable, enjoyable, and a tradition. Plaster angels, shiny tinsel, and brightly colored glass ornaments replaced the edible tree adornments by the end of the 1800s. Such ornaments could be purchased and stored away for use on future Christmas trees. Hazardous lit candles were replaced with electric multicolored bulbs in the twentieth century.

MESSENGER OF LOVE

Listen—be quiet—perhaps you can hear
The Christmas tree speaking, soft and clear:
I am God's messenger of love, and in my Christmas dress,
I come to light your heart and home with joy and happiness.
I bring you pretty packages and longed-for gifts of love,
But most of all I bring you a message from above—
The message Christmas angels sang on that first Christmas night
When Jesus Christ, the Father's Son, became this dark world's light.
For though I'm tinsel laden and beautiful to see,
Remember, I am much, much more than just a glittering tree,
More than a decoration to enhance the Christmas scene,
I am a living symbol that God's love is ever green,
And when Christmas Day is over and the holidays are through,
May the joyous spirit of Christmas abide all year with you.
So have a Merry Christmas in the blessed Savior's name
And thank Him for the priceless gifts that are ours
because He came.

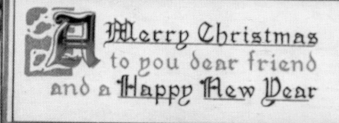

A Merry Christmas to you dear friend and a Happy New Year

CHRISTMAS STOCKINGS

Christmas stockings have been draped on bedposts and "hung by the chimney with care" for generations. One of the first published references to this custom appeared in 1821 in a book for children entitled A New Year's Present. Legend has it, however, that the custom of hanging stockings began in A.D. 300 when word spread of the many kindnesses done by Bishop Nicholas of Myra. After inheriting his family's wealth, the young bishop began leaving gifts for others in need, and he never waited for thanks. He became known as Saint Nicholas, and children began leaving items such as wooden shoes or stockings to be filled with goodies. Parents described the gifts to be left in the stockings or shoes with the saying "One item to eat, one item to read, one item for play, and one item that you need." "One item to eat" was often a pretzel, which originated with Italian monks years earlier. They made the twisted and baked cracker as a reward for children who learned their prayers. The pretzel represented arms folded in prayer. The word pretzel is derived from the Latin pretiola meaning a small gift and pracciatello meaning little arms folded in prayer. In the section "The Making of Gifts at Christmas," learn how the traditional pretzel can be made into a modern holiday treat.

Years ago, the hours shared in games and fun activities were valued more than the gifts that were exchanged. Before television was invented, conversations and parlor games frequently served as forms of entertainment. Of course, children enjoyed skating, sledding, snow games, and tobogganing depending on the weather, but other forms of entertainment were also accessible. Pantomimes using elaborate stage effects and playing characters such

MERRIMENT OF CHRISTMAS

A MERRY CHRISTMAS

as Harlequin, Columbine, and Mr. Punch were popular, as were activities such as the Children's Christmas Tableaux and the Christmas play, a dramatic production written, acted, and staged by the children in the family. Parlor games included charades, Hunt the Slipper, blindman's bluff, Dumb Crambo, and the Christmas umbrella game. Believe it or not, kissing games such as Shy Widow and Postman's Knock were also frequently played at Christmas parties.

CHRISTMAS PUDDING

Christmas pudding, often called plum pudding, was made
popular by George I in the eighteenth century. At
that time, the most essential ingredients—dried
fruits—were known as dried plums. The ingredi-
ents for Christmas pudding were usually assembled
on the Sunday preceding the start of Advent. On "stir-up
Sunday," each member of the household took a turn stirring the
mixture. Decorated with holly and aflame with ignited brandy,
the Christmas pudding was considered the high point of the
Christmas dinner. Additional favorite holiday fares included
trifle, custard sauce, and brandied fruit.

In 1881, Bernard Mayer designed and manufactured candy boxes and containers, some in the shape of cornucopias. After the sweets were eaten, the containers were saved as keepsakes. In 1905, Myers and Sons marketed their religiously decorated paper candy containers as gift boxes to be filled and distributed to students by Sunday school teachers. When tinsel handles were attached, the cornucopia quickly became an ornament for the Christmas tree.

Throughout the 1800s, candy businesses developed at a rapid pace in the United States. By 1850, licorice, cinnamon penny candies, sourballs, and hard candies shaped like ornaments for the tree were very popular.

Red and white striped candy canes also appeared on the scene, the shape reminiscent of the crooks carried by shepherds and, when inverted, a J for Jesus. An age-old interpretation of the traditional red and white candy cane explains the significance of the colors and the stripes. The red symbolizes the blood of Jesus, shed to replace the sins of humankind with a purity as white as snow. The bolder stripe represents belief in one God, and the three thin stripes serve as a reminder of the Holy Trinity: Father, Son, and Holy Spirit.

The Marvels
of Christmas

Among my flowers I have come to see
Life's miracle and its mystery,
And standing in silence and reverie,
My faith comes flooding back to me.

FRANKINCENSE AND MYRRH

A merry Christmas

Frankincense and myrrh, two of nature's gifts, were also two of the gifts presented to the Christ Child by the three wise men. Both frankincense and myrrh come from trees. Frankincense is a hardened resin from the sap of the frankincense tree. Today, incense used in many religious celebrations is made from frankincense and resin from the spruce fir tree. Myrrh comes from the sap of a spiny shrub related to the frankincense tree. In Christ's time, the aromatic, gummy substance from this shrub was an important ingredient in luxurious perfumes and incense and was essential in preparing bodies for burial.

GARLANDS AND WREATHS

The use of boughs of evergreens and garlands of green as holiday decorations goes back centuries. At the Jewish Feast of Tabernacles evergreen branches were one of the main adornments. During the Saturnalia festival, Romans trimmed their homes and shrines with garlands of greens and fruits. The use of greenery was adopted by the Christians as a remembrance of Jesus Christ's deity and everlasting life. The wreath, placed on the heads of heroes, poets, and victors in Greek and Roman times, became a symbol and reminder of the crown of thorns worn by Christ.

The members of the Della Robbia family of Florence, Italy, were known in the fifteenth century for their enameled terra-cotta wreaths that encircled art works depicting the Virgin and Child or a nativity scene. The wreaths contained sculpted flowers, fruits, and pine cones. These Della Robbia wreaths were the inspiration for present-day wreaths that decorate doors, mantels, and tables.

HOLLY WREATHS

When holly wreaths are hanging
upon each friendly door
And candles glow from windows
and trees are trimmed once more,
It's pleasant to be sending
this special wish to you
For all the season's happiness
in everything you do.

Advent Wreath

Christmas trees and candle-light, Make the Christmas Season bright! Merry CHRISTMAS to you!

The Advent wreath is believed to have originated in Germany. It is made of greens twined around a circular metal frame with equally spaced holders for four candles and a place in the middle of the wreath for a large candle. A purple ribbon encircles the wreath. The four outer candles, three purple and one pink, represent the four weeks of preparation leading to the celebration of the birth of the Christ Child. A purple candle is lit on the first three Sundays, and the pink candle is lit on the fourth, or joyful, Sunday. The large, white center candle, the Christ candle, is lit on Christmas Day. Special prayers and devotions accompany the lighting of the candles.

MISTLETOE

The romantic significance attached to mistletoe had its origin in an ancient myth involving Apollo, his mother, Venus, and an evil spirit. Apollo received from Venus a charm that was to protect him from fire, water, air, and earth. The evil spirit, knowing that mistletoe, a parasitic evergreen plant, was not included in any of the aforementioned elements, fashioned an arrow from the plant and shot Apollo. Venus's tears became the white berries on the mistletoe. The myth concluded happily when Apollo was restored to life and Venus announced that never again would mistletoe be used as a weapon. Instead, it would be used in a loving manner, for she would bestow a kiss on anyone who walked beneath a sprig of it. This ancient myth led to the custom of kissing under the mistletoe. For each kiss bestowed, a white berry was to be removed from the hanging sprig. When all the berries were removed, the spell was broken and no more kisses were exchanged. Pity the young maiden who walked beneath a berry-less sprig of mistletoe because, according to the legend, she would not marry that year!

A Merry Christmas

DESIGN COPYRIGHTED, JOHN WINSCH, 1913.

POINSETTIA

The poinsettia serves as a symbol of Christmas in America. Dr. Joel R. Poinsett was appointed the first American minister to Mexico in March 1825, and discovered the plant while there. At that time, the flower that the world has come to know as the poinsettia was considered a native weed by those living in Mexico. Legend tells of the story

of a Mexican maiden who was deeply saddened because she had no flower to place at the manger scene on Christmas Eve in honor of the Virgin Mary and Christ Child, as was the custom of all village folk. While approaching the church, she knelt to pray, picked some weeds, and placed them at the feet of the statue of the Virgin and Child. Instantly, the weeds were transformed into brilliant scarlet blossoms and thereafter were called the Flower of the Holy Night by Mexicans (Flor de la Noche Buena). The plant was brought to the United States in 1836 through the efforts of Dr. Poinsett. Botanists recognized the plant as a rare flower, Eiphorbia pulcherrima. In honor of the South Carolinian who served as the first American minister to Mexico, the botanists named the plant poinsettia. The flower of the poinsettia consists of tiny gold and red blossoms clustered in the center of colored leaves varying in shades of white, pink, and red. These colored leaves are often mistakenly identified as the petals.

The Mystery of Christmas

WITH BEST WISHES FOR A VERY MERRY CHRISTMAS

Christmas is a yearly reunion in heart and in thought,
Renewing the friendships and joys life has brought.

HEART GIFTS

It's not the things that can be bought
that are life's richest treasures—
It's priceless little courtesies
that money cannot measure.
It's some little act of graciousness
or some kindly, little favor
That fills the heart with gratitude
and leaves memories to savor.

Christmas Greeting

THE MAGIC OF LOVE

Love is like magic and it always will be,

For love still remains life's sweet mystery.

Love works in ways that are wondrous and strange,

And there's nothing in life that love cannot change.

Love can transform the most commonplace

Into beauty and splendor and sweetness and grace.

Love is unselfish, understanding, and kind,

For it sees with the heart and not with the mind.

Love is the answer that everyone seeks—

Love is the language that every heart speaks.

Love is the message that was sent to the earth

On that first holy Christmas that heralded Christ's birth.

GIFT OF LOVE

A HAPPY CHRISTMAS.

Christmas be gladdened by joy's
brightest ray,
And nothing but happiness
meet you to-day.

To speak, to act, to work with love

Is something we know little of—

Love that transcends all comprehension

And knows no limit or dimension,

Love that is bigger than the land

And much too great to understand,

Love reaching to the world's far ends

Transforming strangers into friends.

What greater gift could Christmas bring

Than love that touches everything—

A love so meaningful and wide,

The whole wide world is wrapped inside.

THE MYSTERY OF CHRISTMAS

The wonderment in a small child's eyes,

The ageless awe in the Christmas skies,

The nameless joy that fills the air,

The throngs that kneel in praise and prayer—

These are the things that make us know

That men may come and men may go,

But none will ever find a way

To banish Christ from Christmas Day,

For with each child there's born again

A mystery that baffles men.

A Season of Kindness

May the kindly spirit of Christmas

spread its radiance far and wide

So all the world may feel the glow

of this holy Christmastide.

Then may every heart and home

continue through the year

To feel the warmth and wonder

of this season of good cheer.

And may it bring us closer

to God and to each other

'Til every stranger is a friend

and every man a brother.

MERRY CHRISTMAS, FRIEND OF MINE

GREETING CARDS

In 1843, artist John Calcott Horsley designed the first commercially printed Christmas card at the request of a London businessman who desired to send holiday greetings to his friends. The message of the card emphasized the virtue of assisting the poor, but a number of temperance members objected to the card because some of the individuals depicted were holding wineglasses and toasting to a happy New Year.

Henry Cole, the first director of the Victoria and Albert Museum, encouraged the sending of Christmas cards in 1846. By the end of the century, the large number of cards being mailed prompted the postmaster general to request that the public "post early for Christmas delivery." During the Victorian era, the holiday penny postcard was popular. Robins, holly, mistletoe, and snow scenes were favorites, and even unseasonable scenes and spring flowers were featured.

The practice of sending Christmas cards increased in the United States in 1875 when German immigrant Louis Prang of Boston published his own line of colorful and artistic greeting cards. Prang's early Christmas cards, similar in theme to those used in England, contained humor, flowers, elegantly attired ladies, children, and scenes unrelated to Christmas. Many early Christmas cards resembled valentines, with lace, ribbons, and fabric. Some cards were ornate and included a tab or ribbon that when pulled revealed a message of love, trust, health, and happiness.

Prang is recognized for popularizing greeting cards with religious scenes. In the 1960s in America, Helen Steiner Rice wrote religious themed verses on cards published by Gibson Greetings, Inc. Her poem "The Priceless Gift of Christmas" is as popular today as when it was introduced on the 1960 Lawrence Welk television program.

Christmas Wishes

Meine Kindlein, lasset uns nicht lieben mit Worten, noch mit der Zunge, sondern mit der That und mit der Wahrheit. 1 Johannis 3. 18.

NEW YEAR GREETINGS

JOHN WINSCH, 1911.

FRÖHLICH

Xmas Greetings.

Happy New Year

BEST CHRISTMAS WISHES

DESIGN COPYRIGHTED, JOHN WINSCH, 1914.

WEIHNACHTEN

A Greeting Card

A greeting card is more than a pretty design,
More than just words in a rhyme-metered line,
More than just paper and printer's ink—
A greeting card is a heart-to-heart link
Between acquaintances we've met,
Between dear friends we can't forget,
And always a link of love
Between the folks we're fondest of.
Hearts are made a little lighter
And darkest days a little brighter
By greeting cards that play a part
In lighting candles in the heart.

GREETING FRIENDS

It's Christmas and time to greet you once more,
But what can I say that I've not said before
Except to repeat at this meaningful season
That I have a deeply significant reason
For sending this greeting to tell you today
How thankful I am that you passed my way.

Too Nice to Forget

I wonder if you know the real reason
I send you a card every year at this season.

Do you think it's a habit I just can't break

Or something I do just for custom's sake?

I think I should tell you it's something more,

For to me Christmas opens the friendship door,

And I find myself reaching across the year

And clasping the hand of somebody dear.

To me it's a link I wouldn't want broken

That holds us together when words are unspoken,

For often through the year we have to forego

Exchanging good wishes with those we know.

But Christmas opens the door of the heart,

And whether we're close or far apart,

When I write your name I think of you

And pause to reflect and always renew

The bond that exists since we first met

And I found you somebody too nice to forget.

CHRISTMASTIME IS FRIENDSHIP TIME

A HAPPY CHRISTMAS.

At Christmastime our hearts reach out
    to friends we think of dearly,
And checking through our friendship lists,
    as all of us do yearly,
We stop a while to reminisce
    and to pleasantly review
Happy little happenings
    and things we used to do.
And though we've been too busy
    to keep in touch all year,
We send a Christmas greeting
    at this season of good cheer.
So Christmas is a lovely link
    between old years and new
That keeps the bond of friendship
    forever unbroken and true.

The Music of Christmas

Music is something indefinable,
like sea and sky and sod,
It might just be enchantment,
but I like to think it's God.

CAROLING

Christmas carols have been with us since the birth of Christ. The first Christmas carol was sung by a chorus of angels to shepherds in the fields of Bethlehem on the night Jesus was born.

The tradition of caroling was practiced in early times by strolling minstrels and then by English night watchmen who sang as they made their rounds. After night watches were discontinued, caroling was continued by those who strolled the streets singing for their own enjoyment or for the enjoyment of those listening. The custom of carolers going door to door began in America in the mid to late 1800s. In Victorian times, singing groups would trudge through the snow going from house to house. Top-hatted gentlemen in long overcoats and woolen scarves, and ladies wearing bonnets and wrapped in warm capes sang the glad tidings of the season.

Many well-known traditional carols have survived the test of time. The first American Christmas carol, "Jesous Ahatonhia" ("Jesus Is Born"), was written in 1641 by Father Jean de Bre'beuf, a French Jesuit missionary and martyr, for the Huron Indians in Quebec. The Jesuit priest adapted the tune of the French carol "Une Jeune Pucelle" ("A Young Maiden"). He felt confident that the Hurons would respond to the stories from the Bible if the message was made understandable. In a sincere effort to explain the birth of Jesus Christ, he composed "Jesous Ahatonhia" and wrote the carol in the difficult language of the Huron Indians. Documentation verifies that the carol was sung at the mission of Saint Marie in 1641 and of Saint Ignace in 1648.

Hark! The Herald Angels Sing

Charles Wesley was the eighteenth of nineteen children born to Rev. and Mrs. Samuel Wesley. While Charles and his brother John were students at Oxford, they became members of a club designed to strengthen their minds through study and discussion. Later, because the two brothers insisted on particular methods of worship, they were designated the "methodists."

Charles had a special talent for composing hymns including "Love Divine, All Loves Excelling." In 1739, he wrote the lyrics to "Hark! the Herald Angels Sing" with a melody other than the one with which we are familiar. In 1855, William Cummings combined the lyrics of Wesley with a melody written earlier by Felix Mendelssohn.

Hark! the herald angels sing,
"Glory to the newborn King;
Peace on earth, and mercy mild,
God and sinners reconciled!"
Joyful, all ye nations, rise,
Join the triumph of the skies;
With th'angelic host proclaim,
"Christ is born in Bethlehem!"
Hark! the herald angels sing,
"Glory to the newborn King!"

CHARLES WESLEY

JOY TO THE WORLD

Isaac Watts, a pastor of a Calvinist church, wrote "Joy to the World" in the early 1700s. Two of his other well-known hymns are "When I Survey the Wondrous Cross" and "O God, Our Help in Ages Past." One of Watts's favorite Scripture passages was Psalm 100. Watts was so inspired by this psalm, which begins with the line "Make a joyful noise unto the LORD," that he wrote a hymn based on it that indeed expresses great delight, happiness, and praise for the coming of the Lord. Isaac Watts passed away in 1748 while residing at the estate of one of his wealthy parishioners. He had been invited as a guest for a weekend visit and had stayed for over thirty-five years!

Joy to the world! the Lord is come.
Let earth receive her King;
Let every heart prepare Him room,
And heaven and nature sing,
And heaven and nature sing,
And heaven, and heaven and nature sing.

ISAAC WATTS

O Come, All Ye Faithful

There is a question as to the authorship of this beautiful carol. Many authorities attribute it to St. Bonaventure, a French monk and faithful follower of St. Francis of Assisi. Other researchers point to John Francis Wade as the composer. It is known that the hymn was written originally in Latin in the mid 1700s for use at midnight mass services of the Catholic church.

O come, all ye faithful,
   joyful and triumphant,
O come ye, O come ye
   to Bethlehem!
Come and behold Him,
   born the King of angels!
O come, let us adore Him,
O come, let us adore Him,
O come, let us adore Him
Christ the Lord.

AUTHOR UNKNOWN

Go, Tell It on the Mountain

A traditional American folk song passed from generation to generation and sung with great jubilation is the ever popular "Go, Tell It on the Mountain." As with so many folk songs, the origin of this song remains unknown. It is thought to be a spiritual from the early 1800s, passed on by the slaves who believed that the birth of a Savior, who would set all men free, was indeed a miracle worthy of celebrating in song.

What more appropriate location than a mountain from which to spread the good news: God revealed His name and His commandments to Moses on Mount Sinai, Solomon's temple was built on Mount Zion, and Jesus delivered one of His most well-known sermons on a mount in Galilee. And who will ever forget Gethsemane on the Mount of Olives?

The Jubilee Singers of Fisk University popularized this song in 1879 as they traveled the United States and Europe while on a tour to raise money for scholarships for students at Fisk University, which was founded to educate freed slaves.

Go, tell it on the mountain,
Over the hills and everywhere;
Go, tell it on the mountain
That Jesus Christ is born!
While shepherds kept their watching
O'er silent flocks by night,
Behold throughout the heavens
There shone a holy light.
Go, tell it on the mountain,
Over the hills and everywhere;
Go, tell it on the mountain
That Jesus Christ is born!

TRADITIONAL FOLK SONG

SILENT NIGHT! HOLY NIGHT!

According to legend, the hymn "Silent Night! Holy Night!" was written out of necessity by Father Joseph Mohr on Christmas Eve 1818 because the organ in the priest's church was in need of repair. In order to have music for the Christmas mass at St. Nicholas Church in Oberndorf in the Austrian Alps, Father Mohr wrote the beautiful lyrics and decided that a guitar would be used as the alternate instrument. Franz Gruber, a music teacher in neighboring Arnsdorf, wrote the music. The organ repairman heard the song and told a Tyrolean folk singing group about it. The group learned it and eventually sang it for German royalty. From there it circled the globe and is still appreciated around the world.

Silent night! Holy night!
All is calm, all is bright
'Round yon virgin mother
    and child!
Holy infant so tender
    and mild,
Sleep in heavenly peace,
Sleep in heavenly peace.

JOSEPH MOHR

It Came upon the Midnight Clear

Best Christmas Wishes.

The year 1850 was indelibly impressed on the heart, mind, and life of Edmund H. Sears, an ordained minister and pastor of the Unitarian Church in Wayland, Massachusetts. It was the year he married Ellen Bacon of Barnstable, Massachusetts, and the year he composed a hymn that would continue to be sung even a hundred years after his passing.

It came upon the midnight clear,
That glorious song of old,
From angels bending near the earth
To touch their harps of gold:
"Peace on the earth, good will to men,
From heaven's all gracious King!"
The world in solemn stillness lay
To hear the angels sing.

EDMUND H. SEARS

O Little Town of Bethlehem

In 1865, Phillips Brooks, a twenty-nine-year-old American, traveled by horseback from Jerusalem to Bethlehem. The climax of his journey took place when he attended a Christmas Eve service in the Church of the Nativity. Three years after Brooks returned to the United States, the vivid memory of his visit to the land where Jesus was born remained in his heart and mind. At age thirty-two, Dr. Brooks, rector of the Church of the Advent and Holy Trinity in Philadelphia, wrote the words to "O Little Town of Bethlehem" for the children of his Sunday school. His organist, Lewis Redner, provided the music and stated that he was divinely inspired to do so. Dr. Brooks later became the Bishop of Boston.

O little town of Bethlehem,
How still we see thee lie!
Above thy deep and dreamless sleep
The silent stars go by;
Yet in thy dark streets shineth
The everlasting Light—
The hopes and fears of all the years
Are met in thee tonight.

PHILLIPS BROOKS

Away in a Manger

For many years, credit for writing this much loved and frequently vocalized hymn was given to Martin Luther. It was believed that he composed it for his children. Although Luther wrote many beautiful hymns, it has never been verified that "Away in a Manger," sometimes identified as "The Cradle Song" or "The Children's Carol," is one of them. Regardless of the true authorship, this song remains one of the most popular and best loved Christmas carols.

Away in a manger, no crib for a bed,
The little Lord Jesus laid down His sweet head;
The stars in the bright sky looked down where He lay,
The little Lord Jesus, asleep on the hay.

AUTHOR UNKNOWN

The Meditations of Christmas

Help us all to realize
there is untold strength and power
When we seek the Lord and find Him
in the meditation hour.

A Christmas Prayer

MERRY CHRISTMAS

God bless you at Christmas

And go with you through the year,

And whenever you are troubled

May you feel His presence near.

May the greatness of His mercy

And the sweetness of His peace

Bring you everlasting comfort

And the joys that never cease.

A Child's Prayer

Hear me, Blessed Jesus, as I say my prayers today,

And tell me You are close to me and You'll never go away.

Tell me that You love me like the Bible says You do,

And tell me also, Jesus, I can always come to You

And You will understand me when other people don't,

And though some may forget me, just tell me that You won't.

Jesus, stay real close to me at home and school and play,

For I will feel much braver if You're never far away.

And sometimes when I'm naughty, I hope You won't be sad,

For really I don't mean to do anything that's bad.

Most of all, dear Jesus, it's Your birthday, and I know

Our Father sent You to us to live on earth below

So little children like myself would know You too were small

And that You are our dearest Friend and that You understand us all.

Jesus, I like Christmas and the presents that it brings,

But I know Your love is greater than all the other things,

And someday when I'm older, I will show You that it's true

That even as a little child my heart belonged to You.

If we keep Christ in Christmas,

He will keep us every day,

And when we are in His keeping

and we follow in His way,

All our little, earthly sorrows,

all our worries and our cares

Seem lifted from our shoulders

when we go to God in prayer.

Keep Christ in Christmas

A Prayer for Christmas

Merry Christmas to you.

God, give us eyes this Christmas
   to see the Christmas star,
And give us ears to hear
   the song of angels from afar.
And with our eyes and ears attuned
   for a message from above,
Let Christmas angels speak to us
   of hope and faith and love—
Hope to light our pathway
   when the way ahead is dark,

To sing through stormy days
   with the sweetness of a lark,
Faith to trust in things unseen
   and know beyond all seeing
That it is in our Father's love
   we live and have our being,
And love to break down barriers
   of color, race, and creed,
To see and understand and help
   all those who are in need.

Silent Night, Holy Night

Let us listen in silence so we may hear
The Christmas message more clearly this year.
Silently the green leaves grow,
In silence falls the soft, white snow,
Silently the flowers bloom,
In silence sunshine fills a room,
Silently bright stars appear,
In silence velvet night draws near,
And silently God enters in
To free a troubled heart from sin.
For God works silently in lives,
For nothing spiritual survives
Amid the din of a noisy street
Where raucous crowds with hurrying feet
And blinded eyes and deafened ears
Are never privileged to hear
The message God wants to impart
To every troubled, weary heart.
So let not our worldly celebrations
Disturb our Christmas meditations,
For only in a quiet place
Can we behold God face to face.

May the holy remembrance of the first Christmas Day

Be our reassurance Christ is not far away,

For on Christmas He came to walk here on earth,

So let us find joy in the news of His birth,

And let us find comfort and strength for each day

In knowing that Christ walked this same earthly way.

He knows all our needs and He hears every prayer,

God Is Always There

And He keeps all His children always safe in His care,

And whenever we're troubled and lost in despair,

We have but to seek Him and ask Him in prayer

To guide and direct us and help us to bear

Our sickness and sorrow, our worry and care.

So once more at Christmas let the whole world rejoice

In the knowledge He answers every prayer that we voice.

O God, our help in ages past, our hope in years to be,
Look down upon this present age and see our need of Thee,
For in this age of unrest, with danger all around,
We need Thy hand to lead us to a higher, safer ground.
We need Thy help and counsel to make us more aware
That our safety and security lie solely in Thy care.
And so we pray this Christmas to feel Thy presence near
And for Thy all-wise guidance throughout the coming year.
First, give us understanding, enough to make us kind,
So we may judge all people with our hearts and not our minds.
Then give us strength and courage to be honorable and true,
And place our trust implicitly in unseen things and You.
Help us when we falter and renew our faith each day
And forgive our human errors and hear us when we pray,
And keep us gently humble in the greatness of Thy love
So someday we are fit to dwell with Thee in peace above.

A Prayer for God's Continued Help

Best Christmas Wishes.

A Prayer for Peace

Oh, Father up in heaven,
    we have wandered far away
From the holy little Christ Child,
    who was born on Christmas Day—
And the promise of salvation that God
    promised when Christ died
We have often vaguely questioned,
    even doubted and denied.
We've forgotten why God sent us
    Jesus Christ, His only Son,
And in arrogance and ignorance
    it's our will, not Thine, be done.
Oh, forgive us our transgressions
    and stir our souls within,

And make us ever conscious that there is no joy in sin,
And shed Thy light upon us as Christmas comes again,
So we may strive for peace on earth and goodwill between all men.
And, God, in Thy great wisdom, Thy mercy and Thy love,
Endow us with the virtue that we have so little of,
For unless we have humility in ourselves and in our nation,
We are vain and selfish puppets in a world of automation,
And with no God to follow but the false ones we create,
We become the heartless victim of a godless nation's fate.
Oh, give us ears to hear Thee and give us eyes to see,
So we may once more seek Thee in true humility.

A Christmas Prayer of Praise

Praise God, the holy One,

For giving us His only Son

To live on earth as mortals do

To draw us closer, God, to You.

Praise the Father for all things

And for the message Christmas brings.

This is indeed the day of days

To raise your voice in prayers of praise—

For we would have nowhere to go

When life has ended here below,

For redemption came and salvation was won

Through Jesus Christ, the Father's Son.

Bless Your Loved Ones

"Our Father, who art in heaven,"

  hear this Christmas prayer,

And if it be Thy gracious will,

  may joy be everywhere—

The joy that comes from knowing

  that the holy Christ Child came

To bless the earth at Christmas

  for Thy sake and in Thy name.

And with this prayer there comes a wish,

  that these holy, happy days

Will bless your loved ones everywhere

  in many joyous ways.

The Making of
Gifts at Christmas

Hearty Christmas Greetings

Pray for a purpose to make life worth living,
And pray for the joy of unselfish giving.

THE THREE WISE MEN

The first gift giving in celebration of the birthday of Jesus was done by the three wise men when they presented their gifts of gold, frankincense, and myrrh to the Christ Child in the manger. The Magi, or wise men from the East, are identified as Balthasar, Caspar, and Melchior. In presenting their gifts to the Christ Child, the three kings were acknowledging Him as

the King of Kings! The first gift, precious gold, was associated with the authority of kings, and its shiny brightness represents the everlasting Light of the World—Jesus. The second gift, the rare resin, frankincense, was burned at holy and sacred occasions. The third gift, myrrh, another rare resin, was used by the Hebrews in preparing the dead for burial and was a prediction of the death of Christ.

A Gift of Joy

As once more we approach the birthday of our King,

Do we search our hearts for a gift we can bring?

Do we stand by in awe like the small drummer boy,

Who had no rare jewels, not even a toy

To lay at Christ's crib like the wise men of old,

Who brought precious gifts of silver and gold?

But the drummer boy played for the infant Child,

And the Baby Jesus looked up and smiled,

For the boy had given the best he had,

And his gift from the heart
   made the Savior glad.

Today He still smiles
   on all those who bring

Their hearts to lay
   at the feet of the King.

Not in Getting but in Giving

Golden Sheaves,
Nor small. Nor few!
This is my New Years
wish for you!

Only what we give away
Enriches us from day to day,
For not in getting but in giving
Is found the lasting joy of living.
For no one ever had a part
In sharing treasures of the heart
Who did not feel the impact of
The magic mystery of God's love.
And love alone can make us kind
And give us joy and peace of mind,
So live with joy unselfishly
And you'll be blessed abundantly.

LEGENDS OF GIVING

SANTA CLAUS

Santa Claus, pictured in America as the jolly, red-clothed distributor of gifts, has roots going back many years. In the fourth century, the patron saint of children was Saint Nicholas, the Bishop of Myra, who was always accompanied by his valet, Zwarte Piet. The two of them, Nicholas, attired in his bright red bishop robes astride his gray horse, and Zwarte Piet, walking at his side, traveled the streets spreading joy and gifts to those in need. According to legend, they once passed by the home of three young maidens who desperately needed money for dowries. As the young ladies' washed stockings hung by the fireplace to dry, Nicholas dropped in some gold coins—the very answer to their prayers. The popularity of Nicholas spread throughout Germany, Switzerland, and the Netherlands. Stockings were hung on December fifth so that Saint Nicholas would leave gifts on December sixth, his feast day. This custom was brought to New York by the Dutch and quickly spread throughout the United States, becoming part of the Christmas celebration.

OTHER LEGENDARY GIFT GIVERS

In the United States, Santa Claus represents the spirit of giving at Christmastime. Throughout the world, the gift bringer has many different names and even different days of arrival.

In England, youngsters send their letters of hoped-for gifts to Father Christmas, while those residing in Finland anticipate the arrival of Joulupukki and his elves.

Juvenile believers in France leave snacks and a glass of wine for Pe're Noël's arrival on Christmas Eve. In some areas of France, it is Petit Noël, an angelic-looking child, who is thought to bring the gifts.

Christkindl, an angelic messenger of the Christ Child, delivers the Christmas gifts in many areas of Germany. Parlor doors are locked until after the Christmas Eve dinner so that Christkindl has time to decorate the tree and leave presents. Weihnachtsmann, a slim version of Santa Claus, is also known as the gift bringer. He too arrives on Christmas Eve.

Mexican children enjoy the coming of Pancho Navidad, who brings a piñata filled with candies and small treasures. Festivities start nine days before Christmas with a religious representation of the journey made by Mary and Joseph.

Children in the Netherlands anticipate the arrival of Sinter Klaas on a horse. On December 5th, the evening before the feast day of St. Nicholas, Dutch children place their wooden shoes by the fireplace. The shoes contain hay for Sinter Klaas's horse, but before morning, the hay is replaced with tiny presents for the youngsters.

Other legendary gift givers include La Befana in Italy, Star Man and St. Nicholas in Poland, Babouschka and Grandfather Frost in Russia, Julenisse in Scandinavia, and Samichlaus in Switzerland.

The ABC's of Sharing Gifts

Some of the most appreciated and memorable gifts cost no money, require no fancy wrappings, and eliminate the bustling in and out of crowded stores. They are heart gifts and require only that you apply the ABC's of sharing.

Appreciate acts of kindness and accomplish some yourself

Be thoughtful of everyone: family members, neighbors, workers, clerks

Calm someone's fears

Dedicate some of your energy to helping others

Encourage those around you and express your thanks to God

Forgive an intentional or unintentional slight against you

Give away a smile

Hang some food on a tree for God's feathered friends

Include someone who feels lonely

Judge not until all the facts are in

Keep your promises

Love life and laugh a lot

Mend a saddened heart and make a memory

Narrate a story to children

Organize a treat for senior citizens and offer a prayer for peace

Patch a quarrel and praise often

Quit complaining but question injustices

Respond softly to all inquiries and regenerate your spiritual goals

Serve a meal to those in need and solve a problem for someone

Take time to be thoughtful, kind, and gentle

Utilize your talents

Visit an incapacitated friend or new mother and verbalize your willingness to help

Wake up each morning with a smile and a happy, positive attitude

Xmas is an abbreviation for Christmas. The Greek letter chi, shaped like the X in our alphabet, is the first letter of the Greek word Christos, meaning Christ. Never abbreviate your love for Christ and faith in Him. Keep Christ in Christmas.

Yearn to accomplish what God has in mind for you to do

Zealously zero in on a worthwhile charitable project

Rose Potpourri

A sachet or jar filled with homemade rose potpourri is a nostalgic gift that is both fun to make and a delight to receive. The technique and idea were popular in olden days, but the end product is still appreciated today.

INGREDIENTS

6 cups of dried rose petals
1/2 cup dried mint flakes
1/2 teaspoon ground cloves
1/2 teaspoon ground cinnamon
1/2 teaspoon ground allspice
1 1/2 tablespoons orrisroot*

*Orrisroot may be purchased at any pharmacy.

DIRECTIONS

Save the freshest blossoms from a variety of fragrant roses. Separate the petals and spread them in a single layer on a dry cloth or in the lid of a shallow cardboard box. Place in a dry, shady place for a few days until the petals are completely dried. Combine the spices and the orrisroot in a clean glass container with a tight fitting lid. Add the dried rose petals to the spice mixture. Mix well. A few drops of an oil-based fragrance may be added to enhance the fragrant aroma, but it is not essential. Cover tightly. Set aside for a month but remember to stir the contents every few days. Keep the container covered between stirrings. After a month, divide the potpourri into amounts appropriate for individual sachets or small containers. Tie each with ribbon or lace.

Bright
be Your
CHRISTMAS TIDE.

"The people that
walked in darkness have
seen a great light."
Isa IX. 2.

Darkness deep o'er spread
the land,
Sudden burst of Seraph bright,
Brings to Earth the
glorious news
"Jesus comes to give
you light!"
Cecilia Havergal.

SUNBEAMS.

POMANDERS

Pomanders are air fresheners made and used centuries ago. Fragrant and practical, a pomander is fun to make for your own use or as a gift.

MATERIALS REQUIRED
a firm apple, lemon, lime, or orange
a package of whole cloves
ground cinnamon
orrisroot*
an awl or skewer
scraps of netting
ribbon
small silk flowers
a brown paper bag

*Orrisroot may be purchased at any pharmacy.
It is not essential, but it helps to preserve the pomanders.

DIRECTIONS
Wash and dry the fruit of your choice. With the awl or skewer poke randomly spaced holes in the fruit. Insert a whole clove in each hole. Measure equal parts of cinnamon and orrisroot into the bag. The amount used will be based on the number of pomanders being made. Place the clove studded fruit in the bag. Shake well so that the fruit is well coated by the dry ingredients. Open the end of the bag and place the bag with fruit and spices in a dark, dry but cool area. Permit the fruit to shrink and harden. Check at intervals. Rotate fruit so that it dries uniformly. This usually takes three to four weeks. Cut a square of netting large enough to encircle the pomander. Pull the sides of the netting up and tie with a piece of ribbon. Add a silk flower. Tie securely leaving a loop of ribbon long enough to permit hanging in a closet.

FRIENDSHIP TEA

On a chilly night while reading and relaxing by the fireplace or after coming indoors following the fun of ice-skating or tobogganing, a cup of hot friendship tea warms a person. The warmth it creates is outdone only by the warmth of the heart when friendship tea is given as a gift.

INGREDIENTS
2 cups powdered orange breakfast drink mix
3/4 cup instant tea
3 oz. instant lemonade mix
1/2 cup sugar (or equivalent sweetener)
1 1/2 teaspoons ground cloves
2 teaspoons ground cinnamon

DIRECTIONS
Mix all ingredients in a large mixing bowl. Blend well. Spoon into washed and dried gift jars. Place a piece of colorful material on the lid, and tie it in place with a piece of yarn. Attach a label with directions for using:

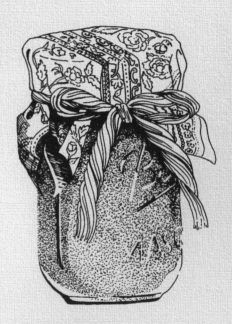

To serve, add 2 to 3 teaspoons of mixture to one cup of hot water.

Red-Nosed Reindeer Snacks

Youngsters enjoy making "pretzel reindeers" for a special holiday treat. Children, teenagers, and adults enjoy eating these snacks!

INGREDIENTS
white chocolate, melted
traditionally shaped pretzels
thin pretzel sticks broken into pieces to create antlers
small, round, colored candies for eyes
red candies, one per reindeer for nose
wax paper

DIRECTIONS
For each reindeer head, spoon approximately 1 tablespoon of the melted white chocolate on a sheet of wax paper. Spread quickly into small circle. While the chocolate is still warm, place a large pretzel in the center of the melted chocolate. Place pretzel stick pieces on top for antlers. Add two candies for the eyes and one red candy for the nose. Work quickly before the chocolate hardens. An adult should supervise the melting of the chocolate for young snack makers.

THE PRICELESS GIFT OF CHRISTMAS

Now Christmas is a season for joy and merrymaking,
A time for gifts and presents, for giving and for taking,
A festive, friendly, happy time with shoppers on their way—
But have we ever really felt the greatness of the day?
For through the centuries, the world has wandered far away
From the beauty and the meaning of the holy Christmas Day,
For Christmas is a heavenly gift that only God can give—
It's ours just for the asking for as long as we shall live.
It can't be bought or bartered, it can't be won or sold,
It doesn't cost a penny, and it's worth far more than gold.
It isn't bright and gleaming for eager eyes to see,
It can't be wrapped in tinsel or placed beneath a tree.
It isn't soft and shimmering for reaching hands to touch,
Or some expensive luxury we've wanted very much.
For the priceless gift of Christmas is meant just for the heart,
And we receive it only when we become a part
Of the kingdom and the glory that are ours to freely take,
For God sent the holy Christ Child at Christmas for our sake
So we might come to know Him and feel His presence near
And see the many miracles performed when He was here.
And this priceless gift of Christmas is within the reach of all—
The rich, the poor, the young and old, the greatest and the small,
So take His priceless gift of love—reach out and you'll receive—
And the only payment that God asks is just that you believe.

What Christmas Means to Me

Christmas to me is a gift from above,
A gift of salvation born of God's love.
For far beyond what my mind comprehends,
My eternal future completely depends
On that first Christmas night centuries ago
When God sent His Son to the earth below.
For if the Christ Child had not been born,
There would be no rejoicing on Easter morn
For only because Christ was born and died
And hung on a cross to be crucified
Can worldly sinners like you and me
Be fit to live in eternity.
So Christmas is more than getting and giving,
It's the why and wherefore of infinite living.
It's the positive proof for doubting God never,
For in His kingdom, life is forever.
And this is the reason that on Christmas Day
I can only kneel and prayerfully say,
"Thank You, God, for sending Your Son
So that when my work on earth is done,
I can look at last on Your holy face,
Knowing You saved me alone by Your grace."